The Heartbreak: A Teenage Book of Poems

AC Knight

Published by AC Knight, 2022.

THE HEARTBREAK: A TEENAGE BOOK OF POEMS

First edition. December 26, 2022.

ISBN: 979-8215667224

Written by AC Knight.

To anyone with a broken heart, feel it and heal from it.

The Heartbreak...

<u>I've got nothing now</u>
I let you slip away...
My hesitation, procrastination,
lead to this invasion of loneliness
that I am now facing.

I sit and watch you happy...
It's not me you are loving
so I constantly, reluctantly try to
erase you from my memory
although there is no true possibility
that you will be removed permanently

If I could turn back the hands of time...
I'd caress your chest, profess my undying
admiration, nonetheless, then confess that I was
wrong to be so careless, your heart was the only
thing I would cherish, now thoughts I ponder
are pointless.

I want another chance...
A second time to charm, easing you
into my arms, holding you at night
to keep you so warm, moments so
sweet and rare prolonged
I swear my love would

have been unusually far...
from the norm.

You're gone...
Now here I sit dumb founded,
My hesitation, procrastination
allowed it, I'll admit, I'm madly
jealous and I'm proud of it, she
makes you so happy, it makes me
Sick! And I, I allowed this bullshit
I allowed you to slip away,
How fuckin foolish...

<u>Misery+Company=?</u>
Misery loves company
but company isn't sure
about how he feels
about misery.
Company loves to nurture
Misery loves to torture
When company first met
misery it was by mistake
but somehow turned into fate.
Company is confused at this
point because misery can't
live without him
Company can't do it
with misery anymore
so misery is kicked out
the door. Company is by
his lonesome to take a break
from everyone
Misery is left in tears, alone
facing the next few cruel years.
Who can misery love now without
being hurt again?

<u>Scent of A Man</u>
Just wrap your arms around me
and hold me tight
I won't fight,
I will not fight...
Pull me close to your body
and hold me tight
I will not fight,
I won't fight...
Loosen your grip from around
my body
Let me go,
I will go...
Push me away from the core
of your love.
I will go,
cuz you let me go...
Make me forget the
details of your continence
Out of my head,
out of my mind...
Let me forget the
feeling of your touch.
Out of my mind,
out of my head...
There's still a part of you
that lingers on with me
You're everywhere in the air.
Here and there,
here and there...
The smell of you still in my clothes, still in my house.
I can handle the broken heart in my hands,

But what I can't handle is the scent of this man...

<u>She Once Gave You Love</u>
When she was with you, she was happy
Crazy in love, no she was madly
Her only thoughts were of you
Her every smile was because of you

Now it's like she doesn't exist
All because of an unfortunate rift
Never do you stray far from her mind
Sadly, the memories of you, she leaves behind

Could have been you still by her side
The only problem is you suffer from foolish pride
Allowing yourself to secretly suffer
while the one you love finds other lovers

Tell me in what world does that make sense
maybe on mars but not on earth I must insist
She knows who you are inside out
She doesn't know the person you pretend to be now
Everyone goes through changes
That doesn't mean they make the ones they love strangers
A woman can only take so much abuse
Until she wakes up one day only to refuse
Heartache that is continuously thrown
She won't catch it and she's not wrong
After the love fades away, she's treated like nothing
Why lead her on, tell her something

When she finally moves on
That's when your emotions come back on
She cares that he cares
But her feelings/heart are no longer up in the air

A bit confused
but she trusts her decisions, she plans not to lose
This man will treat her better
Even though she doesn't know how long they'll be together
During that time
She plans to forget the days she called him "mine"
Like I said before putting those memories in a box
Now the love he once had is lost.

<u>I Cried, He Cried</u>
Last night I stayed up and cried
Realizing you were no longer by side.
I can only reminisce
About the last time we shared a kiss.
It was sweet, it was passion,
It was the only thing everlasting.
I watched you walk out of my life
Not willing to stay and fight
I watched you turn your back on my tears
Facing reality without love was among my fears
We can't get back to the beginning,
The beginning....
The beginning of that beautiful feeling...
We're in two different places,
Seeing different faces,
Making different connections...
The love we once had is steadily fading
Is there any left worth saving?
Possibilities are always possible
The love of one human being to another is inevitable.
If only you believe, believe...
He doesn't want to admit it,
But last night he cried
He realized I was no longer by his side.

I Dream of Love

I saw u once in a dream...
U were my prince charming
rescuing me from the dragon
guarded dungeon...
U swept me up in your harms
looking me in the eyes so deeply,
I'd forgotten I spent so many years locked
away longing for the day
that your touch will be all I needed
to make my heart float away...
I saw u in a dream once...
You were my Romeo and I was
your Juliet, our eyes met
and love was the only thing that felt right in
our young hearts...
No one wanted to see us together
but to us it didn't matter
as long as we had each other...
My heart couldn't bear to be without u
so I died right along with u
There we laid in death our love
Was never to fade...
I dreamed of u.

.

U took me on the date of a lifetime...
A romantic dinner then to the beach
to watch the sun rise...
I laid on your chest listening to your heartbeat
and realized it was in sync with mine...
Then I began softly crying...
I once dreamed of you being my one and only

baby...
but a dream can never be reality...

<u>Come Back 2 Me</u>
It's been five months and I'm feeling it
The loneliness
When you were here it was almost like we were one
Now you're gone
I can't help but think of your kiss and the touch that came after
Now, nothing matters
I'm missing how you were like my shining knight,
Until I pushed you away with all of the fights.
I know you have nothing but love in your heart,
And my bitterness tore us apart.
I'd do anything to be with you again and live happily,
So baby, come back 2 me.

<u>Our love</u>
One minute you treat me like a pair of new shoes
You kept me polished and always looking new
You love the way I look and feel
Then the next minute you change the deal
Now you wear me all the time and don't keep me shined
I'm tired and unwearable anymore
My soles are torn, my seams unsown
Why did you have to break my heart leaving me tired
and falling apart?
Just like those new pair of shoes
One minute they're good and clean
the next they're old and grimy
just like our love

<u>I'm Missing You</u>
If it seems like I'm not being myself lately
it's because I'm not
Being without you has me in
an extremely uncomfortable spot
When you left me alone
it was like hearing the phones dial tone.
Sitting here listening to myself think
is making me realize your gone like Nsync
I'm just trying to pick the pieces of my heart up
but I don't think I want to put them back
together just for them
to fall apart all over again
If it seems like I'm not my normal self
it's cause I'm not
I'm missing you

<u>Pieces Of My Heart</u>
One by one you should try to pick them up
Don't sit there looking dumb
My heart has been broken, jump, and stumped upon
You say we don't have anything,
To me that's a little extreme,
I could have sworn I heard the words "I love you"
come from your mouth a thousand times
You lied
You forget what goes around comes around
Someday I'll be found
by someone who will appreciate
me
But until then I guess our love will never happen again
Until I restore the pieces of my heart,
One by one you should try to pick them up,
The pieces of me

<u>I Left My Heart in Paris</u>
I left my heart in Paris,
Where it is free to love,
With me it's useless
I left my heart in Paris,
Where it is free to experience romance,
With me it's useless.
I left my heart in Paris,
Where it is free to be open to all who want to love it,
With me it's useless.
I left my heart in Paris,
Where it is free to grow inch by inch,
With me it's useless.
I left my heart in Paris,
Where it is free to create new memories to be cherished,
With me it's useless.
I left my heart in Paris,
Keeping it with me would have been careless.

<u>Incarceration of Love</u>
Locked away
Never to see the light of day
Caged up like an animal
In maximum security like Hannibal
24hr locked down
With my freedom so far unfound
No homely visits
Only the cold shoulders of this prison
Bars surrounding
These four walls slow my breathing
I may be here for life
Or maybe it's the love in my
heart that has given up the fight.

<u>I Give Up</u>
I'm tired, maybe even exhausted
Love is what I used to have, now I've lost it.
I'll put on the infamous fake smile
Secretly crying on the inside all the while
I've forgiven but never forgotten
That's why my appetite for love is rotten.
I can be the friend you kiss, I can be the friend
you miss, but I can never be your girlfriend
That idea is quickly dismissed.
I will not allow myself to be put in that position again
Because I know how things will end.
I lost the hope,
the hope that I can feel for someone once more
It's not the guys I choose to ignore
It's the thought of love I can't conjure,
I hate the very thought of giving a piece of me away,
Having a burst of light in my life then everything fading to gray
to be comforted by friend after friend
only to be left feeling like shit in the end.
It's not fair, not fair at all.
I'm done because I'm tired,
I'm tired because I'm done.
Love couldn't have done me anymore more wrong..

<u>Flatline</u>

What does the organ beating on the left side of my chest mean to you?
Don't you know that it skips a beat every time it's neglected and abused?
It may be an organ, but it feels everything you've presented,
They love, the laughter, the warmth, the pleasure,
The hurt, the pain, the aching, the faking..
Yet you still persistently resent it
I may be going into cardiac arrest
Slowly slipping into an eternal rest
Losing the steady pumping,
losing the steady rhythmic like beat..
Try to steady my breathing,
I'm collapsing,
Try to bring me back to life..
but my last image and breath
was watching you give up and walk away..

<u>The Interview</u>
You put in an application and got the interview
The position you applied for was a place in my heart
Unfortunately you couldn't start
Your resume was unimpressive and you had no reliable references.
You were fired from the very beginning
Please try again next holiday season

The Issue

Baby I appreciate you doing all of the extra work
However, I question the true meaning of my worth
You see, I've been hurt by so many men
Which makes it complicated for me to open up my heart again
I'm a good women...
but I guess the fellas are overlooking
There's nothing you can do to make me feel better
because it seems like my hope doesn't matter
Am I bitter about the past?
Hell yea, because I imagined the shit would last
Am I still angry about my feelings being taken as a joke?
Hell yea, because it seems like he laughed the most
I can't sit here and lie,
But baby, I'm making you pay for the mistakes of another guy
So if you refuse to stay
I can't say I blame ya.
It's like I'm damaged goods
my wiring is now not easily understood.
It's like the hardware is in good condition
but now there are important pieces missing
I can't help but be honest..
It's just in me these days to love less.
Babe, I know you'd give me the world
But what purpose would that serve?
I probably wouldn't know how to trust that it's legit
Because I've fallen for so many tricks
It's obvious that it's a heart you want to give to me,
How can you?
When I'm still searching for the one that was stripped from me
Like I said, you don't have to stay and wait,
Nothing is promised tomorrow or today

Baby, I appreciate the work you put into me
At the end of the day I'm the underlining issue...

<u>Revelation</u>
Somehow you became a figment of my imagination
Now I lay here having another revelation
I was caught up in all the hype
blind to the fact that you would disappear out of sight.
What am I to do with my life now
because it just seems love keeps letting to down
I'll never win this battle that I fight
but I think this war will be fought with all my might
Who am I kidding?
I might just throw in the tile and end up leaving
Are you worth my sanity?
Because the potential you have lacks credibility.
I'm not going to waste my outer and eternal youth
on yet another worthless pathetic dude
Somehow I must leave what was said and done in the past
And move on to something better that will potentially last.
Somehow you became a figment of my imagination
Now I lay here having this revelation.

<u>Terminal</u>
I'm a basket case or something
and I fear there is no overcoming
It's attacking the very fabric of my existence
I don't want anyone to bear witness
to my unfortunate and untimely demise
The doctor told me it was called "Love"
and there was no cure for it except for a prayer above
I was smitten with the terrible news
To fight this battle, what's the use?
It developed from an addiction
an addiction I don't care to mention
My only regret is not letting it go
But I was weak and unable
Now I sit here with a sickness
That is terminal.

<u>Still Very Much</u>
Still very much in love with your lips
Still very much in love with your kiss
Don't really care to hide the facts
Because at this very moment I would love to have you back
Still very much thinking about you
Still very much not desiring anyone new
I can't explain my unpredictable feelings
Or why all of a sudden I'm very forgiving
Still very much wishing you the best in life
Still very much wishing to be your wife
But everything happens for a reason
And maybe you were here for a season
Still very much infuriate with your choice
Still very much can't understand the complicated brains of boys.
So I sit and ask myself why bother?
It could only lead to more insuring trouble
Still wishing things didn't end the way they did
Sure hope my friends can one day forgive.
I can't hold a grudge forever
But I can't live with "we weren't meant to be together"
So for now I'll just leave it alone
And continue to strive on this lonely road
Still very much in love with you,
But how much more waiting do you think I'll do?

<u>Photo</u>
Images,
Images of our happiness,
Clips that I can't forget,
Looking at these pictures
I get emotionally triggered.
They capture our love
And the bliss we once thrived in
Still frames of smiles,
Shining so bright and loud
A photo to remind me
That maybe your love is my destiny

<u>My Addiction</u>
All I need is one kilogram of your love
but that wouldn't be enough to get
me beyond and above
I need a small dosage of your touch
and a small kiss rolled up in a blunt
I need a sniff of your scent
then I'll be on my sexual ego trip
I need that grass called satisfaction
and not those prescribed medications
I need your pill of ecstasy,
along with a needle
full of passion inside of me
Maybe rehab
can prevent a relapse
You're my addiction
and a bad habit I
need to start breaking

Wonder

I wonder if he thinks of me like I think of him
Even though we are no more, I still think of
his soft skin, the warmth of his arms, the tone
of his voice, and the sweet taste of his lips
Like a sky without a cloud, I am lonely
I feel empty since he's has left me
He left me with tears falling from my eyes
like rain falling from the sky
I wonder if he still loves me like he said he would
My heart is still stuck on him
I wonder if he knows he has a hold on me
What I wonder the most is
Would he leave his new girl
for the old one who loves him the most.

<u>Abhor</u>
Do you hate me because I think I understand
what we both need to do is look within
You and I have been through so much mess
we simply didn't try our best
I guess this was inevitable, our demise wasn't a far stretch
I don't want anyone to give us empathy
I hate the fact that I think about you when
I'm supposed to be over you
I love you and I know you feel the same
Both of us can take the blame
I don't mean to hurt or disappoint you
I know you abhor me,
The same feeling goes for you.

<u>One-Way Ticket to Nowhere</u>
We have a one-way ticket to nowhere
You cheat on me and I don't care.
I know I'm going do the same to you,
So why are we in this so called "relationship"
When we put each other through so much shit
Yea, I love you, but I can't be faithful
I know you feel the same
What to do?
I want to leave but I want to stay too.
We're a mess putting each other
through so much stress
The lies, the sex, the lust,
LOOK AT THE TWO OF US!
We've lost three things called
Trust, loyalty, and sanity
I know that our one-way ticket will
Be exchanged for a round trip to love
and happiness but until then, we must
find each other again nevertheless

<u>My Heart</u>
A heart that is broken can never be put back together
The pieces can be reconstructed but it will never be truly fixed
Why does love involve so many tricks?
If it seems like it's true, it can't be
If it seems like it won't work, it will
The power of destiny has always been confusing for me,
But amazing and sad at the same time
Why should I keep trying when all I get is lies?
My heart has been broken and the pieces can never be put back
together.

<u>Obsessed</u>
So hard for you to let go, I know,
But you can't stay stuck on me forever
Because true love is a never
You look at me hoping I notice
But to me your face is out of focus
I know you exist,
But to me you're just another name on my list.
Stop being so obsessed and move on
It's for the best
I'm not trying to be mean,
I'm finally coming clean
Get over me and let me be.

<u>Let Me In</u>
Since you won't let me in your heart,
I guess I'll give up
I can't make you love me the way I love you
You're stuck on doing what's best for you
I must be happy for me.
If it involves letting you go,
That's what I must do
Since you won't let me in your heart,
I should have said no from the start

<u>I Want You in My Life</u>
I hate this, I want to talk to you but I can't
You won't give me a chance,
my anger is too advanced.
How can you stand there and look away from me?
It gets my temperature boiling
I should stop and listen because
I know what I am missing
This is not the way we should be ending
We should still be standing as one,
for many years to come
I don't want you out of my life.

<u>No More</u>
I know you can't do this anymore
I sit and ignore
You always tell me how much you care
But I'm never there.
It's time for you to move on,
You can't keep singing that same old love song
I don't want to cause you feel pain
Our relationship is not the same,
You're not the one to blame
I just don't think you or I can do this anymore,
We can't be anymore.
No more being together,
That kind of love doesn't last forever,
Not no more.

<u>Too Many Mistakes</u>
I have made too many mistakes in my life
It's like I'm some unfaithful housewife.
If I could turn back on my mistakes and face them
I would be able to learn from them
First mistake was falling in love with someone unlike me,
Second mistake was believing it was meant to be
Why do people make mistakes?
Is it what takes you and makes you?
I don't know why,
I don't know why I even try
Maybe that was one of my many mistakes.

<u>Loving</u>
Loving is not a game,
Sometimes you will be left in pain
Loving always causes hurt,
Like a bad stain on a shirt
Loving can be good
But not well understood
Loving is real pain
It's not a game.

<u>They Weren't Long Enough</u>
Those days weren't long enough,
The years were so rough
You remember when you held me in your grasp,
Begging me not to look at the past,
But I did and hated it,
The other girls, the other explored worlds.
I thought I was the only one,
Not one to be played with
I saw the true you
I didn't want to be believe
You begged and begged and pleaded,
I wanted to leave, so I did
Those days weren't long enough,
The years were extremely rough
As I look back on the days
I'm glad you're gone.

<u>A Long Talk Goodbye</u>
I can't stay stuck on you
I need to find someone new
A person who cares about my feelings
And isn't afraid of the emotions that come along with healing
Feelings.
Someone I need to meet must have them.
Yea, someday I hope to meet him.
Seriously I can't stay,
No, get out of my way
What? Do I remember our first kiss?
How can I forget...
I thought you'd never remember it.
No, no I know what you're trying to do
You really don't think I have a clue
I'm leaving,
And I'm going to keep breathing and thriving
Without you of course.

<u>Temporary Love</u>
Like the summer breeze
flowing through the sky
My heart pounds
Like the birds gliding or
the grass mounds rustling,
everyday I wonder did
he send you from above
But then it turns...
The summer breeze
turns into winter storms
And my heart breaks
Like the lightening
hitting the sky
I suddenly die,
It must be a breakup.
I wonder everyday if
you weren't sent from above
But only to be a temporary love.

<u>Remain A Friend</u>
I want you to be my friend,
Not an intimate companion
If you know what's best for us
You'll leave me alone and give it a rest.
Believe me it's for the best
I want a friend who can give a hand
Not a man I kiss and leaves over and over again.
If we remain the way we are,
our relationship won't go far
You see, although we were meant to be
I can't compete with this reality
I love someone else
who is not my best friend
I'm sorry but I need you as a friend
not an intimate companion.

<u>It's Said</u>
What's said is said,
My heart was ripped into shreds.
"We'd be better off as friends"
That dreadful letter read in my hands
It's so hard when I think about you
Once again, something so real seems so to be so untrue
I don't know why I feel this way
There are no more words to say
I guess I was used
That I can't refuse
I guess sometimes
You must deal with the crimes of others.
What's said is said.
Reality slapped me on the head.
First love, the heartbreak, now refusal.
Hopefully this poem will comfort my soul.

<u>Love Too Much</u>
I don't it want to
It won't be true
I don't want to remember
That beautiful day in September
You held me in your arms
I felt the sweat forming in my palms
You tilted my head
I didn't want to be anywhere else except maybe a bed
It had to be love, mixed with heartache
I never wanted to take a break
But it's too late, you "I love you."
You meant it, it was true.
Then again, I don't want it to be true,
It's too late, I already love you.

<u>Sometime, Every time</u>
Sometimes it gets so hard
To think if you now that we're apart.
Every time I wonder
If I've made a complete blunder.
Thinking I love you
When I don't even know what is true.
Thinking we would be together for long
Well, I was seriously wrong.
Sometimes it gets hard to face it
Every time I just want to quit
But I can't stop, I can't stop
Loving you is a dead-end job around the clock.

<u>A Shattered Heart</u>
You don't know what love is
"I love you"
Words so untrue
I remember the lies
You seriously couldn't look me in my eyes
"This has been on my mind for a long time..."
Don't even try...
I wish I could look you in the eyes
And tell you how I feel right now
The hate, the hurt, the shame
You are the one to blame
Don't say you know what love is about
Then turn around and break my heart
because that's not what it's about.
For now, I see the child in you,
I'm glad we're though.

<u>An Unwanted Love</u>
I don't want you in my life,
But somehow, I need you
I don't know if you have a clue,
But I do and don't love you.
Why you seem to linger in my mind
drives me crazy all the time.
I want you out of my dreams,
Yet every time it seems,
You creep right back up on me
It seems to be,
You are an unwanted love,
A love that came from below and above.
I don't want you in my life,
But I need you

<u>Dreaming</u>
Thinking about you on these late summer nights
Makes me realize what I've done
The images keep replaying in my head
Over and over again
It was so wrong.
How could I do something like that and to you,
The sweetest guy I ever knew.
Sitting down and really thinking...
What the hell was I thinking!
No one is more special than you to me,
I hope you can see
I'm really sorry.
You don't have to forgive me,
Just know that I'm always thinking
of you and dreaming too.

<u>Come Back to Me.</u>
When will you come back to me
and hold me in your arms
Your touch is never too much.
When will I see you again?
To gaze deeply into your eyes
Is always a beautiful surprise.
Being away from you gets so hard
we're miles apart
to be next to you again
Is my dream...
When will you come back to me?
To be mine again...

<u>Remember</u>
You remember when I used to love you?
It's a shame because I still do
I never thought something so good
wouldn't turn out the way it should.
If I could, I would change the past.
I remember every little thing
Those beautiful songs you used to sing
And to me...
Baby, I remember when I used to love you
But like John said, "I don't love you, not
Like I used to..."

<u>Hurt</u>

I say this all the time,
I would never hurt you
I can't explain why I did what I did,
But I know it was wrong.
Our love is too strong to be lost like that.
Please say you'll take me back
I would do anything to feel your warmth,
I would do anything to hear your voice.
Believe me, I didn't want to hurt you,
Give me a call and come back soon,
I love you

<u>Crying</u>
Crying is the pain that spills from me
Why I feel this way, I will never know
How can you unknowingly make a person fall in love with you?
That's what I guess I'm going through
I guess I was too dumb to see it
I outsmarted myself with my own charm and wit
Making someone fall in love with me just too blind to see it.
Now he's gone
Out of my life forever
I thought I'd never...
Have to endure such an unwanted pleasure
Crying is pain that spills from my eyes,
Now I realize...
I'm missing you.

<u>You Don't Care</u>
Sometimes I stop and think to
find out if you truly care for me
It amazes me the things I see you do,
they hurt me...
I try my best to be your best
It seems to me that you could care less
Why did you ask me to give my hear to you?
If all you were going to do was make me look like a fool
You left me crying on numerous occasions
I just need a long-awaited vacation,
from your neglect...
Do I live with regret of ever meeting you?
No, but I just get the feeling you don't care about me
Like I do you

The Damage

It never astonishes me as to how my
heart won't listen to my brain
Something told me you were
too good to be the real thing
Now I'm sitting here going insane
I have nothing but your face in my memory bank
I wish someone would rob it because I'm done guarding it
I remember all the thing we used to do
I remember everything you used to say
It makes me sick
that I fell for your little tricks
You made me fall in love with you
Now I'm sitting here with the blues
It never astonishes me as to how I gave my heart to you
But it makes me sick to my stomach...
that I chose you
You've broken me and I don't know what to do
Look at the damaged you've caused

<u>You might as well</u>
You might as well have stepped on it
You might as well have set it on fire
You might as well have ran over it with an 18-wheeler
You might as well have fed it to angry lions
You might as well have left it in ruins
You might as well have ripped it right out of me
If you don't know by now
I'm talking about my heart
And you might as well have literally torn it apart...

<u>Maybe It's Me</u>
I can sit here and lie to you all day
You and I both know you weren't born yesterday day
The truth is I can't help that fact that I cheat
Baby maybe it's me
You're a good man and I don't understand
why you stay so stuck to a selfish women
I put myself over your needs
yet you beg for me come back while on your knees
I keep my feelings a secret
and you bear yours for the world to see them
I'm not good for such a king
and everything I do is insulting
Baby maybe it's me.
I am my number one priority
I keep you in the darkest clouds
so I can do my dirt, carelessly being found out
Why won't you let me go
because you and both know I've nothing left to show
I can sit and lie to you all day
but why put you though unnecessary pain
You and I both know I'm the one to blame
Baby we need to call it what it is
there's no need for you to pretend
Maybe baby it's just me
So I have to for once to the right thing by setting you free.

<u>Being Real</u>
I've been here before but
it doesn't feel the same
my heart is slowly breaking
And I'm not sure who's to blame
I care too deeply to simply
let this love die
But it hurts so bad to the point
where it sends unpleasant chills
down my spine
I've come to the point where
I'm unsure if you truly care
You're at a distance yet at the same time
you're physically here
I've come to several conclusions over the past few days
But still my heart is with you, where sadly it will remain
I'm not willing or ready to call it quits
But if you are I'll have to live with it
Love never dies in my book
And second chances are never overlooked
that is if you're willing to give me another try
Because frankly I can't see myself with another guy
I'm trying to make sense of all of my feelings
And begin this process of emotional healing
Like I said, I've been in this position before
But my heart is just too much to ignore
I could seriously hate you for falling in love
But in the end what would that really solve
I'm just saying how I feel
And being me unlike you which is real.

<u>Thinking About You</u>
I'm scared of thinking about you or being next to you.
Although we're over and through, I still feel for you.
If you'd understand me better
we'd still be together
You choose to be with your so-called boys
over my love, affection, and joy
Sometimes I wonder
What if you were more mature?
What if you considered love for sure?
What if you never had those friends?
Would we be together again?
Even though I say such means things
It's never what it seems
I always take them back
That's why I'm scared of thinking about you

<u>Asshole</u>
It wasn't real, not even from the start.
Ok maybe it was but somehow it fell apart
Separate ways we went
lonely days I spent
One minute I meant the world to you
Now you could care less about what I do
Lies are what you present to me and pathetically
Why try to spare my feelings now
when you've already stumped my heart into ground
I question now, Why I ever cared for you?
Why I ever loved you?
Why I ever waited for you?
Why I ever cared?????!
Like seriously?
I could say bluntly now
FUCK YOU and your life
FUCK YOU and your heart,
Obviously, you don't have one...
Are my feelings a fucking joke?
My answer is no
I love hard and I don't like playing with emotions
I expect the same in return, but that's too much to
ask these days because people are so fucking fake
You're not worth everything I can give a man,
You're not worth my heart so please by all means
be with other women
But don't you dare sit here and lie to me,
The people I hate in this world, the phony
Don't touch me, don't hold me
I don't have shit to say to you
FUCK YOU

I don't care anymore, my energy
I've wasted, it's been ignored
I wanted to fight for you but
you're not at all the same dude
people's true colors come out after a while
I was in denial,
I have all the reason to accept it now.
You're an asshole.
always have been,
always will be.
An asshole, a clogged up one
I was willing to wait, wait, and wait.
with no debate
Why you are in life?
I will never understand
God must be showing me the truth
in its rawest form because now
there is no question, I am moving
On to better
You took me for a ride I must admit
took me for a ride, night and day
Let's face it, I have guys coming at me left and right
Why I shut them down?
Because of you, you FUCKING clown
This is the last time I'll be writing about you,
I spare no one's feelings because all I do is spit the truth.
You're an asshole baby, an asshole, and I no longer love you.

<u>Back in the Day</u>
Let's go back to high school and reminisce
Where puppy dog relationships exist
Every couple lives in total bliss
Blind to the real world
they will have to face
trying not to grow up so fast
living at a slow a pace
love that was built up
is now a waste.
College is a totally different place
relationships will be tested
some will survive
And many will fail
A test of power will be present
hurt but they will smile through disaster.
Let's go back to when love was simple.
Let's go back to high school,
So we can remember.

<u>Twisted</u>
When your heart says you want one thing
But you mind says you want another
You feel twisted
Man, times have changed
I might have fell in love and missed it
Twisted...When you're wrapped up in
something and you can't get out of it
you're twisted
Confused, okay that's one way to say it
Confused, you don't know what you want
Should I go with the old or discover something new?
Someway I'll try to fix it, I'm sure
I won't miss it
Man, it's messed up when your mind is twisted.

<u>Poem 3</u>

Never the right time or place
Your emotions are never easy to trace
Leave me alone
I can stand your voice or its tone
You're driving me insane
But I'm addicted to you like cocaine
I can't let you control my existence
Let that power go, you trippin
Never can you express what's inside
Who can I run to in order to confide
that pain and love you continue to provide
Never the right time or place
But I'll continue to hold on and keep you figuratively safe

<u>Tell Me</u>
Tell me a lie because it sounds so much better
Keep your secrets because they are valuable treasures
Make sure your every move is calculated
Make sure when you speak to me, I believe it

Feed me all the tales in your heart
Feed me the idea of love from the start
Make no plans to plan
Because everyone knows for a fact they will not stand

Persuade me with the language of your body
To believe that your mind is where you've got me
Be the person who I want you to be
Not the person you are in reality

Lie to me ever so sweetly
How can you be guilty, just tell me.

<u>Ones Broken Promises</u>
I can't ever say things are going to be the same
promises were made
promises should never be made if only
to be broken
how can you say you'll love me forever
if within five months we won't be together
how can you make me your world
when your eyes slowly turn to watch other girls
why should you believe me when I say
I won't be leaving tomorrow or today
can I love you forever?
yes, but will I promise...never.
I never make's promises I don't intend to keep
then again someone's words are
not to be truly trusted, therefore we call them cheap
it's easy to say, I'll promise to be there for you everyday
but as time passes feelings slowly begin to fade away
then what does your promise entail
a falsehood, unknowingly deception therefore
sending emotions through personal hell
It's funny how one minute a person can
mean the world to you but when
a promise is made and trust is broken
in both of your worlds the other is nonexistent
its hard and a tough decision to let the one
you care for go because of a white lie, a lie
that meant well, but in the end failed to be followed through
ones broken promises
what can you do?
what can be done?
just promise to give the truth a chance

just promise to make a lie sound wonderful in advance
it's true I'll love you forever
even when we are not together
Will you do the same is what I wonder...

About the Author

AC Knight is a Chicago native who's also a United States Navy veteran. She is currently a student at Tidewater Community College pursuing her Associates Degree in General Studies with plans to transfer to a university to obtain her Bachelors studying Journalism and Mass Communication.

Inspired by the late great Maya Angelou, she has always had a passion for writing with plans to release a series of novellas. She resides in Portsmouth, Virginia with her loving husband, daughter and two Siberian huskies.